Science Keywords

THE LIVING WORLD

Karen Bryant-Mole

WAYLAND

Titles in the series

English Keywords – Words and Sentences
Maths Keywords – Numbers and Calculations
Science Keywords – The Living World
Science Keywords – The Material World

All Wayland books encourage children to read and help them improve their literacy. In this book:

✓ The contents page, page numbers, headings and index help children find specific pieces of information.

✓ The layout of the book helps children understand and use alphabetically ordered texts.

✓ The design of the book helps children scan text to locate particular key words.

✓ The structure of the book helps children understand and use non-fiction texts that are made up of definitions and explanations.

If a particular key word has an unusual plural form or appears in a modified form within the text of the book, this form has been shown in brackets.

Design: Jean Wheeler
Cover design: Viccari Wheele
Consultant: Stuart Ball

First published in 1999 by Wayland Publishers Limited, 61 Western Road, Hove, East Sussex BN3 1JD

© Copyright 1999 BryantMole Books

British Library Cataloguing in Publication Data

Bryant Mole, Karen
Science Keywords – The Living World. – (Keywords)
1. Biology – Dictionaries, Juvenile literature
I. Title
570.3

ISBN 0 7502 2415 0

Printed and bound in Italy by Eurografica S.p.a. - Marano

Acknowledgements
The publishers would like to thank the following for allowing their pictures to be reproduced in this book.
(t) = top (b) = bottom
Zul Mukhida: 7(t); 11(b); 13(b); 21(t); 24(t)
Positive Images: 5(b); 6(b); 8(b); 12(t); 16 (t); 18(b), 20 (t); 22(b); 23(t); 27(t); 28(b); 30(b); 31(t)
Tony Stone Images: 4(t) Paul Harrison; 4(b) Robert Brons/BPS; 5(t) Art Wolfe; 7(b) Manoj Shah; 9(t) Michael Busselle; 10(b) Charles Krebs; 13(t) Art Wolfe; 14(t) Pal Hermansen; 14(b) Stuart Westmorland; 15(t) Keren Su; 15(b) Bill Ivy; 16(b) Charles Krebs; 17(b) Rod Planck; 19(t) James Balog; 19(b) Charles Sleicher; 21(b); 23(b) Pal Hermansen; 24(b) Art Wolfe; 25(a) James Balog; 26(t) Marc Chamberlain; 26(b) John Warden; 28(t) Norbert Wu; 29(t) Rob Talbot; 29(b) Renee Lynn; 30(t) Rich Iwasaki; 31 Rod Planck(b)
Wayland Publishers Limited: 6(t); 8(t); 9(b); 10(t); 11(t); 12(b); 17(t); 18(t); 20(b); 22(t); 25(b); 27(b)

Contents

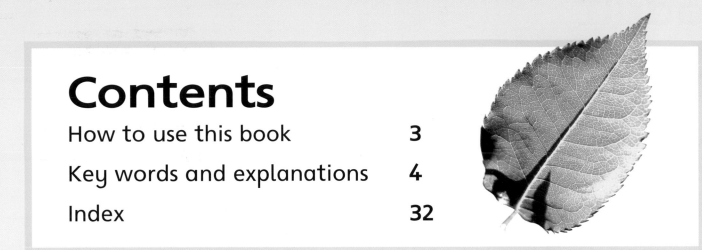

How to use this book

This book is made up of key words. Each key word is printed in **bold** and is followed by an explanation.

• The key words are listed in alphabetical order. The words printed in large letters at the top of the page will help you find the key word you are looking for. The word at the top of each left-hand page is the first key word that appears on that page. The word at the top of each right-hand page is the last key word that appears on that page. Every key word that comes in between those words can also be found on these two pages.

• You will find an index at the back of the book. The index will show you where the explanation of each key word can be found, other pages where that word appears and where you can find any related pictures.

• As you read through an explanation, you will notice that some of the words may be <u>underlined</u>. Each of these underlined words has its own explanation.

Enjoy exploring the Keywords trail!

adult

adult A <u>human</u> or other <u>animal</u> whose body is fully-grown.

air Air is all around us. It is made up of a mixture of <u>gases</u>, including <u>nitrogen</u>, <u>oxygen</u> and <u>carbon dioxide</u>. <u>Animals</u> that live on land and <u>plants</u> use air for <u>respiration</u>. Plants also use air in the <u>process</u> of <u>photosynthesis</u>.

alive Having life. The opposite of <u>dead</u>. Anything that is alive is able to carry out <u>living processes</u>.

amphibian A <u>cold-blooded</u> <u>vertebrate</u> with a soft, damp <u>skin</u>. Amphibians are born in <u>water</u> but spend most of their <u>adult</u> life on land. The young usually look very different to the adults. (See also <u>metamorphosis</u>.)

animal Animals are <u>living</u> things that can <u>move</u>, <u>feed</u>, <u>respire</u>, <u>grow</u>, use their <u>senses</u>, <u>reproduce</u> and get rid of <u>waste products</u>. Animals can be put into different groups, or <u>classified</u>.

anther Part of a <u>flower</u> that is to do with the process of <u>reproduction</u>. It is where <u>pollen</u> is made. The anther is found at the end of the <u>stamen</u>.

aquatic Anything that lives in or near <u>water</u> can be described as aquatic.

▲ The frog is a type of **amphibian**.

▲ The jellyfish is an **aquatic** animal.

artery (arteries) Arteries are tubes inside the body that carry <u>blood</u> away from the <u>heart</u> and take it to different parts of the body. (See also <u>circulation</u>.)

b

baby A very young <u>human</u> or other <u>animal</u>.

backbone Also called the spine. It is made up of 33 smaller <u>bones</u>. All <u>vertebrates</u> have a backbone. <u>Nerves</u> run through the backbone to the <u>brain</u>.

bacterium (bacteria) Special types of <u>micro-organisms</u>. Some are harmful to <u>humans</u> and are often called <u>germs</u>. Other types of bacteria are helpful. Bacteria help <u>dead</u> <u>plants</u> and <u>animals</u> to <u>rot</u>. (See also <u>classify</u> and <u>disease</u>.)

balanced diet A <u>diet</u> that includes <u>fibre</u> and the right amount of <u>nutrients</u> to keep the body <u>alive</u> and <u>healthy</u>.

bark The outside layer of the <u>stems</u> of <u>trees</u> and <u>shrubs</u>. It protects the <u>plant</u> and stops the plant from drying out.

biology The study of <u>living</u> things.

bird A <u>warm-blooded</u> <u>vertebrate</u> with feathers and <u>wings</u>. Birds <u>hatch</u> from eggs. Most birds can <u>fly</u>.

▲ A **baby** elephant, with its mother.

▲ The **bark** of a tree.

5

blood

blood A fluid that is pumped around the arteries and veins of humans and many other animals by the heart. Blood carries nutrients and oxygen to each body cell and takes away waste products such as carbon dioxide. Blood contains special cells that protect the body from diseases. (See also circulation.)

bone Bones make up the skeleton of most vertebrates. Bones are light but strong. A human skeleton is made up of about 206 bones.

botany The study of plants and any other living thing that is not classified as an animal.

brain A group of nerve cells that control the body. The brain is found in the head of humans and many other animals. Messages travel between the brain and all parts of the body. These messages are sent along nerves. The brain also controls memory and thinking.

breathe Take air into the lungs and push air out of the lungs. (See also respiration.)

broad-leaved Broad-leaved trees are flowering plants with wide, flat leaves.

bud Part of a plant. Buds usually grow on stems or branches. Inside buds there may be tiny shoots, leaves and flower parts, waiting to grow. (See also sepal.)

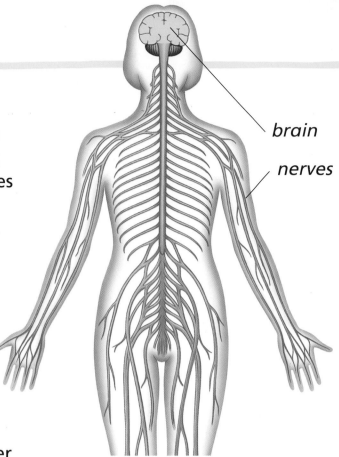

brain

nerves

▲ Messages travel to and from the **brain** along nerves.

▲ The beech is a **broad-leaved** tree.

bulb A special sort of <u>bud</u> that grows underground. It contains <u>food</u> for the <u>plant</u> to help it start to grow.

C

carbohydrates A group of <u>nutrients</u> found in <u>food</u>. Most carbohydrates are types of sugar. Carbohydrates give the body <u>energy</u>.

carbon dioxide A type of <u>gas</u>. It is found in <u>air</u>. All <u>living</u> things give *out* carbon dioxide as a <u>waste product</u> of <u>respiration</u>. <u>Plants</u> take *in* carbon dioxide to use in the <u>process</u> of <u>photosynthesis</u>.

carnivore An <u>animal</u> that <u>feeds</u> mostly on other animals.

carpel The carpel contains the <u>female</u> parts of a <u>flower</u>. Some flowers have one carpel, others have many. The carpel is made up of an <u>ovary</u> and a <u>stigma</u>, which are joined together by a part called a style.

cell All <u>living</u> things are made up of cells. Simple <u>micro-organisms</u> may have only one cell. <u>Humans</u> have billions of cells. There are many different types of cells and all have their own particular job.

▲ Bread, biscuits and potatoes are high in **carbohydrates**.

▲ The leopard is a **càrnivore**.

chlorophyll

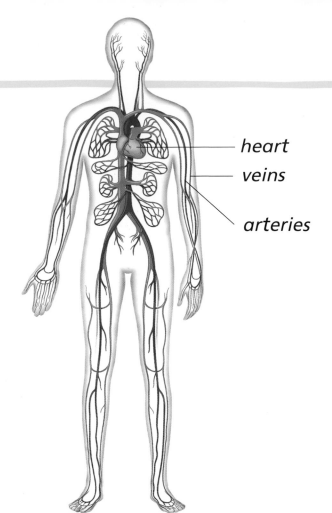

heart

veins

arteries

chlorophyll Chlorophyll is found in the leaves of plants. It soaks up the energy of sunlight, which it uses in the process of photosynthesis.

circulation The movement of blood around the body. The blood is pumped around the body by the heart. (See also artery and vein.)

classify (classified) Put into groups. All living things can be classified. Living things are sometimes put into one of two groups: plants or animals. But some living things do not really belong to either of these groups, so they are often put into one of five groups. These five groups are: plants, animals, fungi, a group that includes bacteria and a group that includes some types of seaweeds.

▲ The main arteries and veins that are to do with the **circulation** of blood in humans.

cold-blooded A cold-blooded animal is an animal whose body temperature changes depending on the temperature of the air or water around it. All amphibians, reptiles and fish are cold-blooded. (See also warm-blooded.)

conifer Conifers are trees with narrow, needle-like leaves. Their seeds develop inside cones. Most conifers are evergreen. (See also plant.)

consumer See food chain.

▲ The pine is a **conifer.**

d

dead No longer <u>alive</u>, having once been a <u>living</u> thing. Once something is dead it is unable to carry out <u>living processes</u>.

deciduous Deciduous <u>trees</u> and <u>shrubs</u> lose all their <u>leaves</u> for part of the year. Most <u>broad-leaved</u> trees are deciduous.

decomposer A <u>living</u> thing that <u>feeds</u> off dead <u>plants</u> and <u>animals</u>, helping them to <u>rot</u>. (See also <u>bacterium</u> and <u>fungus</u>.)

develop <u>Grow</u> and change.

die Stop being a <u>living</u> thing.

diet The sort, and amount, of <u>food</u> usually eaten.

digestion The <u>process</u> of breaking down <u>food</u> that is eaten, so that the body can use its <u>nutrients</u>.

disease Something that stops the body working properly. Diseases usually have a set of signs, or symptoms.

disperse <u>Seed</u> dispersal is the spreading of a <u>plant</u>'s seeds. Different plants disperse their seeds in different ways. For example, some seeds are dispersed by the wind. Some are dispersed by <u>animals</u>.

drug Drugs make changes to the body. They are usually used to stop people getting <u>diseases</u> and to help them if they become ill. (See also <u>medicine</u>.)

▲ Most **deciduous** trees drop their leaves in autumn.

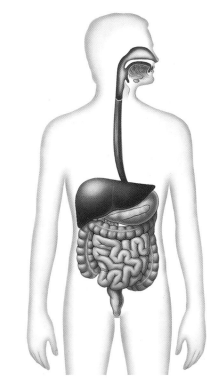

▲ The journey that food makes through the body during the process of **digestion**.

ear

ear The organ that is used by many animals for hearing. Messages are sent from the ear to the brain, along nerves. The brain understands these as sounds. (See also sense.)

▲ Inside the human **ear**.

ecosystem A particular environment and all the plants and animals that live together there.

egg A female sex cell that is to do with the process of reproduction in most animals. An egg is fertilised by a sperm. Some animals, including humans, have eggs that grow inside the body. Others lay their eggs outside the body.

embryo A fertilised egg or ovule develops into an embryo. (See also foetus.)

endoskeleton See skeleton.

energy Living things need energy to grow and to keep every part of them working. Their energy comes from food.

environment A living thing's environment is its surroundings. It includes all the non-living things as well as all the other living things that are around it.

evergreen Evergreens are trees and shrubs that do not lose all their leaves at the same time. Most conifers are evergreens.

▲ These fir trees are **evergreens**.

excretion The <u>process</u> of getting rid of <u>waste products</u>.

exercise Exercise keeps the body fit and <u>healthy</u>. Exercise can, for example, build up strong <u>muscles</u>.

exoskeleton See <u>skeleton</u>.

extinct A <u>species</u> of <u>animal</u> or <u>plant</u> that used to be <u>alive</u> but has now disappeared. The dodo is an extinct animal.

eye The <u>organ</u> that is used by <u>animals</u> for seeing. When light comes into the eye, messages are sent from the eye to the <u>brain</u>, along <u>nerves</u>. The brain understands these as pictures, or images. (See also <u>sense</u> and <u>sight</u>.)

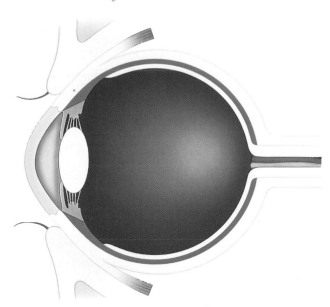

▲ Inside the human **eye**.

f

fats A group of <u>nutrients</u> in <u>food</u>. Fats give the body <u>energy</u> and help to build <u>healthy</u> body <u>cells</u>. If the body has too much of this nutrient, it cannot get rid of it but has to store it.

feed Get <u>nutrition</u> from <u>food</u>.

feel To do with the <u>sense</u> of <u>touch</u>. <u>Humans</u>, and other <u>vertebrates</u>, feel through their <u>skin</u>. Being able to feel pain and heat helps to stop us damaging our bodies.

▲ Cream, butter and cheese are high in **fats**.

female

female Usually describes a <u>living</u> thing that can produce the <u>eggs</u> that are part of the <u>process</u> of <u>reproduction</u>. The word is also used to describe a <u>sex cell</u> that can be <u>fertilised</u> by <u>sperm</u> or <u>pollen</u>.

fertilisation Part of the <u>process</u> of <u>reproduction</u> in many <u>living</u> things, including <u>humans</u>. It is the joining together of a <u>male</u> <u>sex cell</u> and a <u>female</u> sex cell. (See also <u>embryo</u> and <u>pollination</u>.)

fertilise Go through the <u>process</u> of <u>fertilisation</u>.

fibre Sometimes called roughage. Fibre forms part of a <u>balanced diet</u>. It helps to push <u>food</u> through the body.

fin Part of a <u>fish</u>'s body. Fins are used for balance, steering and stopping.

fish An <u>aquatic</u>, <u>cold-blooded</u> <u>vertebrate</u>. Fish have <u>scales</u> and <u>fins</u> and usually <u>respire</u> using <u>gills</u>. Most fish <u>hatch</u> from <u>eggs</u> and <u>move</u> by swimming.

flower The part of a <u>flowering plant</u> where <u>reproduction</u> takes place. Flowers are made up of <u>sepals</u>, <u>petals</u>, <u>carpels</u> and <u>stamens</u>.

flowering plant A <u>plant</u> that produces <u>flowers</u>. Its <u>seeds</u> <u>grow</u> in a <u>fruit</u>. (See also <u>nectar</u> and <u>tree</u>.)

▲ A **female** chicken is called a hen.

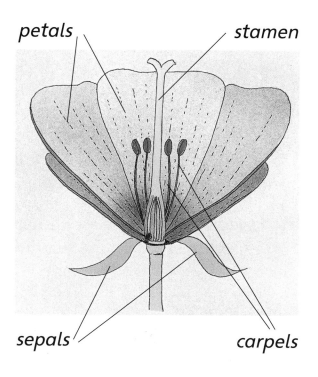

petals   *stamen*

sepals   *carpels*

▲ The main parts of a **flower**.

fluid Something that flows, or is runny.

fly A type of <u>movement</u> through <u>air</u>. <u>Birds</u> fly by flapping their <u>wings</u> or by gliding.

foetus A stage in the <u>process</u> of <u>reproduction</u> in <u>humans</u> and other <u>mammals</u>. It is the stage between being an <u>embryo</u> and being born.

food Food provides <u>living</u> things with <u>energy</u> and helps them to <u>grow</u> and stay <u>healthy</u>. <u>Animals</u> have to find food. The food they eat goes through the <u>process</u> of <u>digestion</u>. <u>Plants</u> make their own food using the process of <u>photosynthesis</u>. (See also <u>diet</u> and <u>nutrient</u>.)

food chain Food chains show how one <u>living</u> thing is eaten by another. For example, foxes eat rabbits which eat grass. Food chains show that all <u>animals</u> depend on <u>plants</u> for their <u>food</u>, even if they themselves do not eat plants. In a food chain, plants are called producers and animals are called consumers.

food web Food webs show how <u>animals</u> in different <u>food chains</u> are linked together.

fruit The name given to the <u>ovary</u> of a <u>flowering plant</u> while the <u>seeds</u> inside it are <u>developing</u>. An apple is an example of a fruit. Many <u>nuts</u> and some of the foods known as vegetables are also fruits.

▲ This eagle can **fly**.

▲ These are all types of **fruit**.

fungus

fungus (fungi) Fungi are a group of <u>living</u> things that includes mushrooms and moulds. They are sometimes <u>classified</u> as <u>plants</u> but they do not have green <u>leaves</u> and cannot make their own <u>food</u>. They <u>feed</u> off <u>dead</u> and <u>rotting</u> plants and <u>animals</u>. Fungi are <u>decomposers</u>.

fur The name given to the thick <u>hair</u> of some <u>animals</u>, such as cats and bears.

g

gas Gases are all around us but cannot usually be felt. They have no shape and can spread everywhere. <u>Air</u> is made up of a mixture of different gases.

germ A name that is sometimes used to describe <u>micro-organisms</u> that cause <u>diseases</u>. (See also <u>bacterium</u> and <u>virus</u>.)

germinate Begin to <u>develop</u>.

gills The <u>organs</u> of <u>respiration</u> in most <u>fish</u> and many other <u>aquatic</u> <u>animals</u>. <u>Water</u>, which is partly made up of <u>oxygen</u>, flows over the animal's gills. Oxygen passes into the animal's <u>blood</u>, while the <u>waste product</u>, <u>carbon dioxide</u>, passes out.

▲ These **fungi** are feeding off rotting leaves.

▲ A curved dark line marks the opening to this fish's **gills**.

grow All living things grow. They get bigger and they may change shape too. Humans and other animals grow all year round. They stop growing when they become adults. Plants do most of their growing at particular times of the year. They continue growing until they die.
Living things need food in order to grow.

h

▲ The panda's **habitat** is the forestland of China.

habitat The place where a plant or animal usually lives.

hair Hair grows from the skin of many animals, including humans. Hair keeps an animal warm by trapping air that is then heated by the animal's body.

hatch Be born from a fertilised egg that has been laid by a female animal.

head The body part that is usually at the front or at the top of an animal. It is where the brain and most sense organs are usually found.

healthy A word used to describe a living thing that is in good condition.
Or something that helps to keep it in good condition, such as a healthy diet.

▲ Baby birds **hatch** from eggs.

hearing

hearing One of the five main <u>senses</u>. It is to do with understanding <u>sound</u>. <u>Humans</u>, and most other <u>animals</u>, hear through their <u>ears</u>.

heart The main <u>organ</u> of <u>circulation</u> in most <u>animals</u>, including <u>humans</u>. The human heart is mostly made up of <u>muscle</u>. It acts like a pump, pushing <u>blood</u> around the body. Each pump of the heart can be heard as a heartbeat or felt as a <u>pulse</u>.

herbivore An <u>animal</u> that <u>feeds</u> mainly on <u>plants</u>, or parts of plants such as <u>seeds</u>, <u>roots</u> or <u>fruits</u>.

human The word that is used in <u>biology</u> to mean a person.

i

insect An <u>invertebrate</u> with a body that has three parts: the <u>head</u>, the thorax and the abdomen. It has two antennae on its head and six legs on its thorax. Most <u>adult</u> insects also have <u>wings</u> on their thorax. During their <u>life cycle</u>, insects go through a <u>process</u> called <u>metamorphosis</u>.

invertebrate Any <u>animal</u> that is not a <u>vertebrate</u>. All <u>insects</u> are invertebrates.

▲ Sheep are **herbivores**.

▲ The ant is an **insect**.

j

joint A place where two movable parts of an animal's body meet. In humans, and most other vertebrates, it is where bones in the skeleton meet. Joints allow the body to move.

k

l

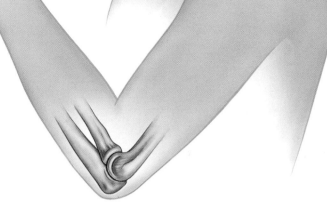

▲ These are **joints** in the human arm and hand.

larva (larvae) Some animals that go through the process of metamorphosis hatch as larvae. The larva looks very different to the adult and usually has a different way of life. Some larva, such as the caterpillar, become a pupa before becoming an adult.

leaf (leaves) Leaves grow on the stems of plants. They are where the plant makes food for itself through the process of photosynthesis. Stomata in the leaf allow the plant to respire. Veins in the leaf carry water and nutrients to all parts of the leaf. There are two main forms of leaf. Simple leaves are made up of one main piece. Compound leaves are made up of several small leaves.

▲ The caterpillar is the **larva** of the butterfly.

life cycle

life cycle Every <u>living</u> thing has a life cycle. It is the set of stages that it goes through from <u>fertilisation</u> to the time when it <u>reproduces</u> and starts the life cycle all over again. In <u>humans</u>, this includes the stages of <u>embryo</u>, <u>foetus</u>, <u>baby</u>, child and <u>adult</u>. The life cycle of some <u>animals</u> includes the <u>process</u> of <u>metamorphosis</u>.

living Is able to carry out <u>living processes</u>.

living processes A set of <u>processes</u> that all <u>living</u> things can carry out. They are: <u>movement</u>, <u>respiration</u>, the use of <u>senses</u>, <u>growth</u>, <u>reproduction</u>, <u>excretion</u> and <u>nutrition</u>.

lungs The main <u>organs</u> of <u>respiration</u> in many <u>animals</u>, including <u>humans</u>. When <u>air</u> is <u>breathed</u> into the lungs, through the <u>nose</u> and <u>mouth</u>, <u>oxygen</u> passes from the air into the <u>blood</u>. At the same time, <u>carbon dioxide</u> passes from the blood back into the lungs and is then breathed out.

male Usually describes a <u>living</u> thing that can produce the <u>sperm</u> that are part of the <u>process</u> of <u>reproduction</u>. The word is also used to describe a <u>sex cell</u> that can <u>fertilise</u> an egg or <u>ovule</u>.

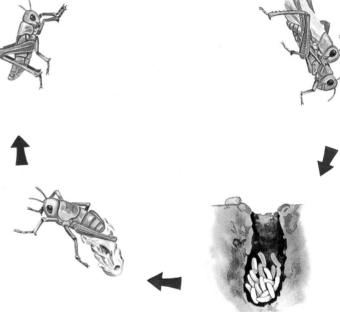

▲ The **life cycle** of the grasshopper.

▲ A **male** chicken is called a cockerel.

mammal A <u>warm-blooded</u> <u>vertebrate</u>. All mammals have <u>hair</u> or <u>fur</u> and <u>feed</u> their young on milk.

medicine Medicines are used to treat <u>diseases</u>. Most medicines are types of <u>drugs</u>.

metamorphosis A <u>process</u> that most <u>amphibians</u>, many <u>invertebrates</u> and some <u>fish</u> go through. During this process, changes happen to the <u>animal</u>'s body. Metamorphosis can be complete or incomplete. In complete metamorphosis, the animal <u>hatches</u> as a <u>larva</u> and may go through a stage as a <u>pupa</u> before <u>developing</u> into an <u>adult</u>. In incomplete metamorphosis, the animal develops into an adult after hatching as a <u>nymph</u>.

micro-organism A tiny <u>living</u> thing that is so small that it can only be seen through a microscope. <u>Bacteria</u> and <u>viruses</u> are types of micro-organisms.

minerals All <u>living</u> things need to take in minerals. <u>Humans</u> and other <u>animals</u> get their minerals from the <u>food</u> they eat. Different minerals have different uses. Some, for instance, help to make <u>bones</u> strong. <u>Plants</u> get their minerals from soil. (See also <u>nutrient</u> and <u>root</u>.)

mini-beast A name that is sometimes given to an <u>insect</u> or other small <u>animal</u>.

▲ These gorillas are **mammals**.

▲ The spider could be called a **mini-beast**.

mouth

mouth An opening, usually in the <u>head</u>, that <u>animals</u> use to take in <u>food</u>. Many animals also use it to take in <u>air</u>.

move Show <u>movement</u>.

movement In <u>humans</u> and other <u>animals</u>, movement usually means the <u>process</u> of travelling from one place to another. Animals need to be able to <u>move</u>, so that they can find <u>food</u> for themselves and keep safe from other animals. Movement can also be to do with a <u>living</u> thing moving parts of itself. <u>Plants</u> cannot move from place to place but they can move parts of themselves. Many plants move their <u>leaves</u> so that they catch as much <u>sunlight</u> as possible.

muscle Muscles are stretchy bundles of <u>cells</u>. They help the body to <u>move</u>. Muscles are often attached to <u>bones</u>. They work by pulling the bones in a particular direction. There are also muscles in many of the body's <u>organs</u>, such as the <u>heart</u> and the <u>eye</u>.

n

nectar A sugary <u>fluid</u> that is made by <u>flowering plants</u> to attract <u>animals</u>. As the animals drink the nectar, <u>pollen</u> may be brushed onto or off their bodies. (See also <u>pollination</u>.)

▲ These plants **move** their petals. They close them up at night.

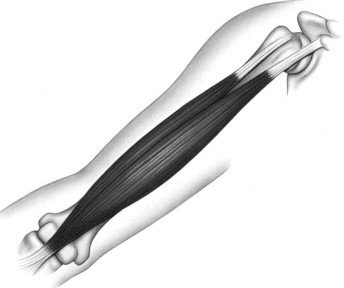

▲ These **muscles** are found in the human arm.

nerve Nerves are bundles of cells that send messages to and from different parts of the body. (See also brain.)

nitrogen A type of gas. It makes up more than three-quarters of the air we breathe.

non-living A name given to something that is not, and never has been, living.

nose The main organ of the body that is to do with the sense of smell. Smells mix with the air and are breathed in through the nose. Messages are sent from the nose to the brain, along nerves. The brain understands these messages as different types of smell.

▲ The acorn is a type of **nut**.

nut A dry fruit. It has a hard shell that contains one seed.

nutrient Anything that feeds a living thing can be called a nutrient. There are several important groups of nutrients. They are: carbohydrates, fats, proteins, vitamins, minerals and water.

nutrition To do with feeding a living thing. (See also digestion and nutrient.)

nymph Some insects hatch as nymphs. A nymph is a young insect that looks similar to the adult. As it goes through the process of metamorphosis and develops into an adult, it gets bigger and grows wings.

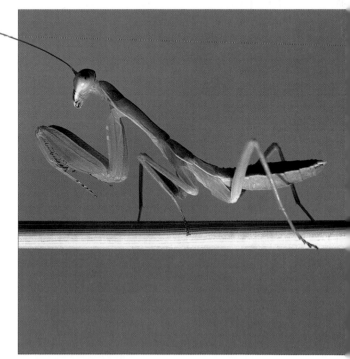

▲ This praying mantis hatched as a **nymph**.

omnivore

omnivore An <u>animal</u> that <u>feeds</u> on <u>plants</u> and on other animals.

organ A particular part of a <u>living</u> thing.

organism A <u>living</u> thing.

ovary An <u>organ</u> that is to do with <u>reproduction</u>. It is where an <u>animal's</u> <u>eggs</u> or a <u>plant's</u> <u>ovules</u> are stored.

ovule Part of a <u>flowering plant</u> that is to do with <u>reproduction</u>. Ovules contain <u>female</u> <u>sex cells</u>. After being <u>fertilised</u> by <u>pollen</u> they become <u>seeds</u>.

ovum (ova) Another word for <u>egg</u>.

oxygen A type of <u>gas</u> that is found in <u>air</u>. <u>Water</u>, too, is partly made up of oxygen. All <u>living</u> things need to take in oxygen to stay <u>alive</u>. (See also <u>respiration</u> and <u>photosynthesis</u>.)

p

petal Petals are parts of <u>flowers</u>. Flowers that are <u>pollinated</u> by <u>animals</u> often have brightly-coloured petals to attract the animals to the flower.

photosynthesis The <u>process</u> used by <u>plants</u> to make <u>food</u> for themselves. <u>Chlorophyll</u>, which is found in <u>leaves</u>,

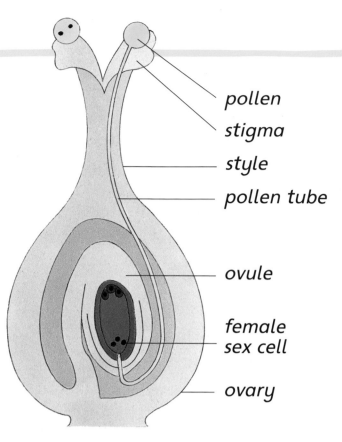

▲ A plant's **ovule** is fertilised by pollen.

▲ This flower has bright yellow **petals**.

uses the energy of sunlight to change carbon dioxide from the air and water from the soil into food.

photosynthesise Go through the process of photosynthesis.

pistil Another word for carpel.

plant Plants are a group of living things. Plants contain chlorophyll and can make food for themselves through the process of photosynthesis. There are two main groups of plants: mosses, and plants that have leaves, stems and roots. This second group is made up of other, smaller, groups. These include: ferns, conifers and flowering plants. Plants are a very important part of the food chain. (See also classify.)

pollen Part of a flowering plant that is to do with reproduction. Pollen contains male sex cells. Pollen is produced in the plant's anther.

pollinate Go through the process of pollination.

pollination The process during which pollen travels from an anther to a stigma of the same type of flowering plant. After this, the pollen grows a tube down into the ovary, where it fertilises an ovule. Some plants can pollinate themselves but usually the pollen has

▲ Mosses form one of the two main groups of **plants**.

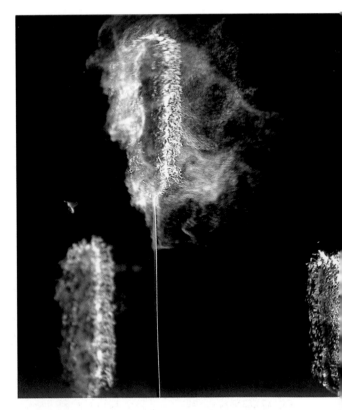

▲ The wind is blowing grains of **pollen** from these grasses.

process

to get from one plant to another.
Some plants are pollinated by the
wind, others are pollinated by <u>animals</u>.
(See also <u>petal</u> and <u>nectar</u>.)

process A set of actions or changes that
happen over a period of time.

producer See <u>food chain</u>.

proteins A group of <u>nutrients</u> in
<u>food</u>. Proteins help to build
<u>healthy</u> body <u>cells</u>.

puberty A time during which body
changes take place in <u>humans</u>. Someone
who has been through puberty is able
to <u>reproduce</u>.

pulse A push of <u>blood</u> as it is pumped
around the body by the <u>heart</u>. This push
can be felt in places where <u>arteries</u> are
near the <u>skin</u>.

pupa (pupae) A stage in the <u>life cycle</u> of
some <u>animals</u> that go through
<u>metamorphosis</u>. The animal usually rests
during this stage, while its body makes
the change from <u>larva</u> to <u>adult</u>. The
chrysalis, for example, is the pupa of
the butterfly.

▲ Meat, fish, eggs and beans
are high in **protein**.

▲ This is the **pupa** of a butterfly.

q

r

reproduce Go through the <u>process</u> of <u>reproduction</u>.

reproduction The <u>process</u> of making more <u>living</u> things of the same kind. All living things can <u>reproduce</u>. If they could not, they would become <u>extinct</u>. Most <u>animals</u> and <u>plants</u> reproduce from <u>sex cells</u>. Some plants and animals can reproduce in other ways. Potatoes, for example, grow fat underground <u>stems</u>, which <u>develop</u> into new plants.

reptile A <u>cold-blooded</u> <u>vertebrate</u>, with <u>skin</u> that is covered with <u>scales</u>. Reptiles <u>hatch</u> from <u>eggs</u> and are born on land.

respiration The <u>process</u> of taking in <u>oxygen</u> from the <u>air</u> or from <u>water</u> and giving out <u>carbon dioxide</u>. It is also called the exchange of <u>gases</u>. Respiration in <u>humans</u>, and many other <u>animals</u> that live on land, takes place in the <u>lungs</u>. In <u>fish</u>, and many other <u>aquatic</u> animals, it takes place in the <u>gills</u>. Plants <u>respire</u> through <u>stomata</u>.

respire Go through the <u>process</u> of <u>respiration</u>.

root Most <u>plants</u> have roots. Roots usually <u>grow</u> underground. They stop the plant falling over. <u>Water</u> and <u>minerals</u> are taken into the plant through its roots.

▲ The snake is a type of **reptile**.

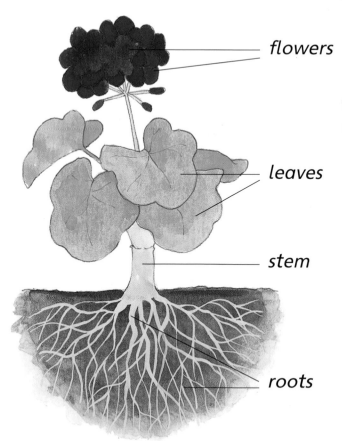

flowers

leaves

stem

roots

▲ A plant is fixed in the ground by its **roots**.

rot

rot Once a living thing is dead, bacteria and fungi start to feed on it. It begins to break down and eventually becomes part of the soil. The process of breaking down is called rotting or decomposing.

S

sap The name given to the fluid that travels around plants, carrying water and nutrients.

scales All reptiles have scales on top of their skin. They help to make the skin more waterproof. The scales may lie next to each other or overlap. Most fish also have scales. Their scales are underneath the top layer of skin.

seed Most flowering plants grow from seeds. A seed develops from a fertilised ovule. Seeds have a hard covering. Inside the seed there is a plant embryo and a food store, which will be used to feed the plant until it grows green leaves and can photosynthesise. (See also disperse.)

sense Humans, and many other animals, have five main senses. These are: hearing, smell, taste, sight and touch. The ear, the nose, the tongue, the eye and the skin are all sense organs. They take in information, which is sent to the brain, along nerves.

▲ Turtles have **scales** that lie next to each other.

▲ These are the **seeds** of the maple tree.

26

sepal Sepals are parts of <u>flowers</u>. They surround and protect the flower while it is a <u>bud</u>.

sex cell A special <u>cell</u> that is to do with the <u>process</u> of <u>reproduction</u>. Sex cells are produced by most <u>animals</u> and <u>plants</u>. In animals, the <u>male</u> sex cells are called <u>sperm</u> and the <u>female</u> sex cells are called <u>eggs</u>. In <u>flowering plants</u> the male sex cells are contained in <u>pollen</u> and the female sex cells are contained in <u>ovules</u>.

shrub A <u>plant</u> that has more than one woody <u>stem</u>. (See also <u>tree</u>.)

sight One of the five main <u>senses</u>. It is to do with being able to see things. <u>Humans</u>, and most other <u>animals</u>, see through their <u>eyes</u>.

skeleton The frame that gives the body its shape and protects its soft <u>organs</u>. Some <u>animals</u>, including <u>humans</u>, have a skeleton that is inside their body. This is called an endoskeleton. Others, including all <u>insects</u>, have a skeleton that is on the outside of their body. This is called an exoskeleton. (See also <u>bone</u>.)

skin <u>Humans</u>, and other <u>vertebrates</u>, have a body that is covered in skin. Skin stops the body from drying out and helps to control its <u>temperature</u> by producing sweat. Skin is the <u>organ</u> of <u>touch</u>.

▲ The buds of these iris flowers are protected by **sepals**.

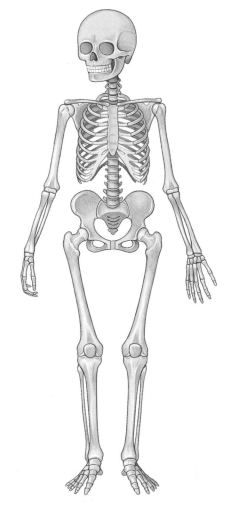

▲ The human **skeleton**.

smell

smell One of the five main <u>senses</u>. <u>Humans</u>, and many other <u>animals</u>, smell through their <u>nose</u>. Smell is closely linked to <u>taste</u>.

sound To do with the <u>sense</u> of <u>hearing</u>. Sound is heard in the <u>ear</u>.

species A particular kind of <u>animal</u> or <u>plant</u>.

sperm A <u>male</u> <u>sex cell</u> that is to do with the <u>process</u> of <u>reproduction</u>. A sperm <u>fertilises</u> an <u>egg</u>.

spine See <u>backbone</u>.

stamen Stamens are the <u>male</u> parts of <u>flowers</u>. They are usually made up of thin stalks, called filaments, with <u>anthers</u> at the end, where <u>pollen</u> is made.

stem A <u>plant</u>'s stalk. Some plants have one stem, others have more than one. New <u>leaves</u>, branches and <u>flowers</u> are produced from the stem. <u>Water</u> and <u>minerals</u> are carried up the stem from the <u>roots</u>. A <u>tree</u>'s main stem is often called a <u>trunk</u>. (See also <u>sap</u> and <u>shrub</u>.)

stigma Part of a <u>flower</u>'s <u>carpel</u>. It is where the <u>pollen</u> lands during the <u>process</u> of <u>pollination</u>.

stomata Tiny openings in the underside of a <u>plant</u>'s <u>leaves</u> through which <u>respiration</u> and <u>transpiration</u> take place.

▲ The dolphin is a particular **species** of animal

▲ This flower has a very long **stamen**.

sunlight All living things depend on sunlight. The sun produces energy by burning gases. Plants need this energy in order to photosynthesise. Without sunlight there would be no plants. Without plants, the food chain would collapse and all living things would die.

t

taste One of the five main senses. Humans, and many other animals, taste through their tongue. Taste is closely linked to smell.

temperature A measurement of how hot or cold something is.

tongue The organ of taste. The human tongue can sense four types of taste: sweet, sour, salt and bitter.

tooth (teeth) Teeth are found in the mouths of many animals, including humans. There are different kinds of teeth. Canines and incisors are used for biting and tearing food. Molars are used for chewing and grinding food.

touch One of the five main senses. It is to do with being able to feel things.

transpiration Plants lose water through their stomata. This loss of water is called transpiration.

▲ Butterflies can **taste** through their feet.

▲ Lions have **teeth** that are good for tearing.

tree

tree A plant that has one woody stem (or trunk) which is covered in bark. Some trees are flowering plants. Some are conifers. (See also shrub.)

trunk The name given to the woody stem of a tree. The word is also used to mean the main part of a human's body.

u

v

vein Veins are tubes inside the body which carry blood from the body back to the heart. The word also means the parts of a plant's leaf that water and food travel along. (See also circulation.)

vertebrate An animal that has a backbone. All mammals, reptiles, amphibians, birds and fish are vertebrates.

virus Viruses cause diseases. Measles is a human disease caused by a virus. Many viruses can be passed from one living thing to another.

vision Another word for sight.

vitamin All animals need vitamins. They are usually taken in in food. There are

▲ This is a maple **tree**.

▲ The lines you can see in this leaf are its **veins**.

several different types of vitamin. Without enough of each, the body can become damaged.

W

warm-blooded A warm-blooded <u>animal</u> is an animal whose body <u>temperature</u> stays the same, no matter how warm or cold the <u>air</u> or <u>water</u> around it. <u>Humans</u> are warm-blooded. (See also <u>cold-blooded</u>.)

waste product Something that a <u>living</u> thing makes but does not need. <u>Carbon dioxide</u> is an example of a waste product.

water Water is important to every <u>living</u> thing. All living things, including <u>humans</u>, are mostly made up of water. Water is lost from our bodies when we <u>breathe</u>, sweat or go to the toilet. This water has to be replaced through <u>food</u> and drinks. <u>Plants</u> need water in order to <u>photosynthesise</u>.

wing The body part of some <u>animals</u> that allows them to <u>fly</u>. <u>Birds</u>, bats and most <u>adult</u> flies and beetles have two wings. Adult butterflies, moths, wasps, bees and dragonflies have four wings.

▲ The cat is a **warm-blooded** animal.

▲ Dragonflies have four **wings**.

X   **y**   **z**

Index

The numbers that are printed in **bold** show the pages of the main explanations.
The numbers that are printed in *italics* show the pages where there are pictures.

A word may appear in more than one explanation on any one page.